Seashore

Lucy Beckett-Bowman
Designed by Caroline Spatz

Illustrated by Patrizia Donaera

Additional illustrations by Tim Haggerty

Seashore consultant: Andy Horton, British Marine Life Study Society
Reading consultant: Alison Kelly, Roehampton University

Contents

Beside the Sea

The seashore is where the land meets the sea. There are different types of seashore all over the world.

This is a sandy beach. Sand is made from tiny pieces of broken shell and rock.

Turning tides

When the seashore is covered in water, it is called high tide. When the shore is bare, it is called low tide.

High and low tide happen twice a day.

Plants and animals live high up the seashore. They can survive both in and out of the water.

Blennies are fish that can live out of water.
Their slimy bodies help them slide over rocks.

At low tide most of the shore is uncovered.
Some parts are always underwater.

Rocky pools

At low tide, pools of water are sometimes left between rocks.

The pools are full of life. Crabs, mussels and little fish live in them.

A sea anemone lives on a rock in a pool. It waves its tentacles to attract fish.

If a fish touches the tentacles it is stunned by a powerful poison.

The anemone guides the fish to its mouth in the middle of its body.

Boxer crabs hold stinging sea anemones to defend themselves from attack.

Shiny seashells

Many seashore creatures have shells covering their bodies.

Scallops swim by pushing out water as they open and close their shell.

Nautiluses grab food with their long tentacles and pull it inside their shell.

Abalones have strong shells that are hard for other creatures to break.

Hermit crabs don't grow a hard shell like most crabs. They find another creature's old shell and crawl inside it.

When this crab gets too big for this shell, it will leave it and find a bigger shell.

Plant life

Plants that live at the seashore have to survive strong winds, and salty air and water.

Sea holly has thick leathery leaves, that don't get torn by powerful winds.

Thrift grows between rocks high up the shore, so that salty water can't reach it.

Sea kale has long roots that reach down to find fresh water below ground.

Marram grass has leaves that roll up to trap damp air inside, so they don't dry out.

Portland spurge stems have a nasty taste. This stops rabbits from eating them.

Seaweed

Seaweed is a type of plant that grows underwater at the seashore.

Some seaweed has pods called air bladders in its fronds, or leaves. The pods are full of ai and make the fronds float under the water.

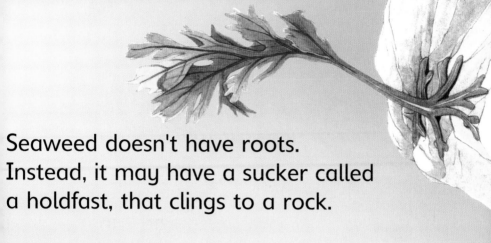

Seaweed doesn't have roots.
Instead, it may have a sucker called
a holdfast, that clings to a rock.

Most seaweed has a slimy layer
that stops it from drying
out at low tide.

When the tide comes in, seaweed floats
upright and its fronds spread out.

Flying feeders

Many birds live at the seashore because there is lots of food for them to eat.

Gannets fly over the water and then dive to catch fish.

Oystercatchers use their long beaks to pull worms from the sand.

Turnstones flick over stones with their beaks to look for food.

When seabirds drink too much sea water, they get rid of it through their noses.

Birds build nests and lay eggs by the seashore.

This puffin has collected sand eels to feed to its babies.

Up and under

At the seashore, many animals spend time both on land and in the sea.

Mudskippers breathe through gills when they are swimming. On land, they breathe through their wet skin.

Sea otters hold their breath when they dive underwater to look for food.

A sea otter picks up a mussel and then finds a large stone.

It swims to the surface and balances the stone on its tummy.

The otter smashes the mussel's shell against the stone.

It pulls out the mussel with its teeth and eats it.

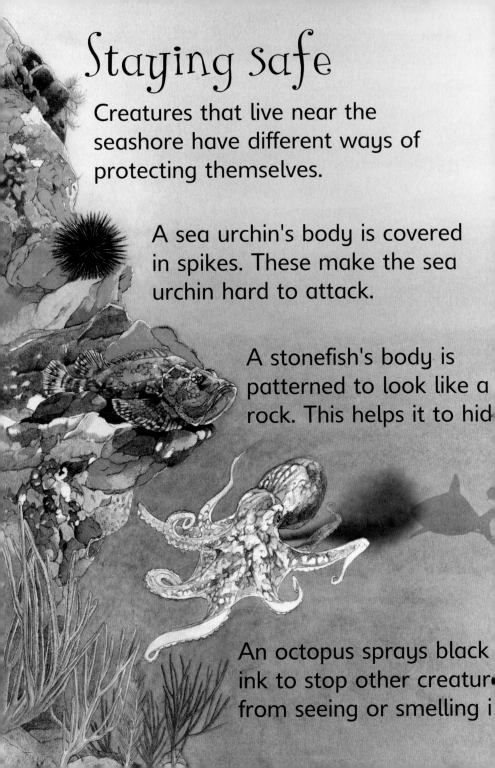

Staying safe

Creatures that live near the seashore have different ways of protecting themselves.

A sea urchin's body is covered in spikes. These make the sea urchin hard to attack.

A stonefish's body is patterned to look like a rock. This helps it to hid

An octopus sprays black ink to stop other creatur from seeing or smelling i

When a pufferfish is in danger, it sucks in lots of water to make itself bigger.

If a crab tries to eat a sea cucumber, it may get sprayed with long sticky threads.

Beach babies

Most sea turtles spend their lives swimming in the sea, but they come onto a beach to lay their eggs.

A mother turtle digs a hole in the sand.

She lays about 100 eggs in the hole.

She then buries the eggs with sand.

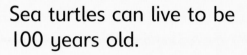

Sea turtles can live to be
100 years old.

When baby turtles hatch out of their eggs,
they dig their way out of the sand and
crawl to the sea.

Making waves

Most waves are caused by the wind blowing across the surface of the water.

On a calm day the wind blows gently. Small waves ripple across the water.

When it is stormy, the strong wind makes huge waves crash onto the shore.

Over many years,
the waves carve away
the land, making tall cliffs.

The huge rocks in the sea
were part of the land, until
waves wore away the rock
between them.

Coral reefs

In some hot parts of the world, large
reefs of coral grow in shallow water
by the seashore.

Corals grow in different
shapes. Some have branching
'fingers', and some are
flat like a plate.

Lionfish hunt in reefs. They trap little fish against the coral with their long fins.

Parrotfish eat coral. They have special teeth that look like a hard beak.

Cool coasts

Some seashores are very cold. The creatures that live there have special ways of coping with the freezing sea.

Seals have a thick layer of fat, called blubber under their fur. This keeps their bodies warm.

Blubber covers their whole body except their head and flippers.

Penguins dive into the icy sea to hunt for food.

They must keep swimming or they will freeze.

Their bodies are covered in oily feathers that keep water out.

Most seabirds fly to warmer places when the weather gets too cold.

Seashore treasures

There are lots of interesting things that get washed up onto the seashore.

This is a Man O' War.
It's like a jellyfish.

It has an air bladder that makes it float in the water. This Man O' War has been blown onto a beach by strong winds.

Small dogfish
and rays lay their
eggs inside an egg case.

 Sand dollars are the shells
of round, flat sea urchins.
They look a bit like coins.

Whelks lays lots of eggs
in egg cases. When they
are empty, they look
like this.

On the sea bed, precious pearls grow inside
some oyster shells. They are very rare.

Glossary of seashore words

Here are some of the words in this book you might not know. This page tells you what they mean.

 tentacles - long thin parts of a sea creature.

 scallop - a small creature that lives in a shell.

 air bladders - pods filled with air that make seaweed and jellyfish float.

 fronds - long pieces of leaf-like seaweed that float in the water.

 gills - part of a fish that helps it to breathe underwater.

 coral - lots of tiny animals, called polyps, that live in warm seas.

 blubber - a thick layer of fat that keeps many sea creatures warm.

Websites to visit

If you have a computer, you can find out more about the seashore on the internet. On the Usborne Quicklinks Website there are links to four fun websites.

Website 1 - Watch a video of scallops swimming.

Website 2 - Play a game about rocky pools.

Website 3 - Discover lots more about sea otters.

Website 4 - Try a fun seashore game.

To visit these websites, go to **www.usborne-quicklinks.com** Read the internet safety guidelines, and then type the keywords "beginners seashore".

The websites are regularly reviewed and the links in Usborne Quicklinks are updated. However, Usborne Publishing is not responsible, and does not accept liability, for the content or availability of any website other than its own. We recommend that children are supervised while on the internet.

Seagulls live on seashores all over the world.

Index

Acknowledgements

Series Designer Zoe Wray
Series Editor Fiona Watt
Art director Mary Cartwright

Photographic manipulation by John Russell

Photo credits
The publishers are grateful to the following for permission to reproduce material:
© John W. Banagan/Getty Images 23; © Jane Burton/naturepl.com 16; © Digital Vision 21;
© R. Dirscher/Frank Lane Picture Agency 24-25; © M.D. Guiry/algaebase.com 12;
© Don Haddon/ardea.com 9; © Martin Harvey/Alamy 1; © Steven Hunt/Getty Images 19;
© mediacolor's/Alamy 31; © Jose B. Ruiz/naturepl.com 10; © John Russell Cover background, 10, 26, 31;
© Steffen & Alexandra Sailer/ardea.com 26; © Iain Sarjeant/Oxford Scientific 2-3;
© Seapics.com 21; © Lynn M. Stone/naturepl.com Cover; © Kim Taylor/naturepl.com 15;
© Stuart Westmorland/Getty Images 28

Every effort has been made to trace and acknowledge ownership of copyright. If any rights have
been omitted, the publishers offer to rectify this in any subsequent editions following notification.

Sun, Moon and Stars

Farm animals

Elizabeth I

Trash and Recycling

Dogs

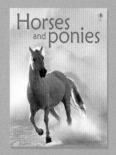

Horses and ponies

Spiders

Planes

Ancient Greeks

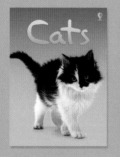

Cats

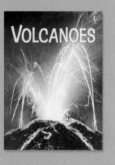

Volcanoes

Dinosaurs

Your Body

Armor

Sharks

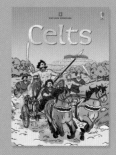

Celts

Vikings

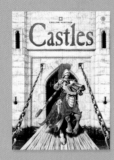

Castles

How flowers grow

Knights

Living in space

Caterpillars and Butterflies

Ballet

Pirates

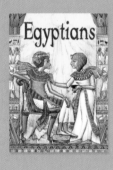

Egyptians

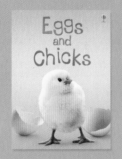

Eggs and Chicks

Romans

Weather

Tadpoles and frogs

Why do we eat?

Under the sea

Bears